THE TEACHINGS OF PTAHHOTEP

The Oldest Book in the World

Edited by Brittany Starr

First published Circa 2388 B.C. Fifth
Kemetic (Egyptian) Dynasty under the
title:

Teachings of the Prefect of the City. Dja Ptahhotep under the
majesty of the King of the South and the North Assa Died-Ka-
Ra, living eternally forever,

TABLE OF CONTENTS

.

Introduction

Ptahhotep was a vizier in ancient Egypt who was known for his influential wisdom literature. The teachings in this book emphasize the importance of humility, faithfulness to one's own duties, and that silence really can be golden. One of the major reasons why this book is so interesting is because it shows that Black people actually wrote in that time period. Furthermore, these teachings were originally written in hieroglyphics which demonstrates the fact that we had our own writing style and language as well. In addition, this proves that there are written records showing how civilized and accommodating to one another Black people were since the beginning of time. The teachings of Ptahhotep are what I like to call the original ten commandments.

These are instructions by the Mayor of the City who is also the Vizier. His name is Ptahhotep and he serves under Pharoah Assa who lives for all eternity. The Mayor of the City, Vizier Ptahhotep, addressed the Supreme Divinity, the Deity as follows:

"God upon the two crocodiles." (Refer• ence to Heru) who is sometimes shown standing on two crocodiles. My God, the process of aging brings senility. My mind decays and forgetful- ness of the things of yesterday has already begun. Feebleness has come and weakness grows. Childlike one sleeps all day. The eyes are dim and the ears are becoming deaf. The strength is being sapped. The mouth has grown silent and does not speak. The bones ache through and through. Good things now seem evil The taste is gone. What old age does to people in evil is every thing. The nose is clogged and does not breath. It is painful even to stand or to sit. May your servant be authorized to use the status that old age af• fords, to teach the hearers, so as to tell them the word^of those who have listened to the ways of our ancestors, and of those who have listened to the Gods. May I do this for you, so that strife may be banned from among our people, and so that the Two Shores may serve you?

Then the majesty of the Deity said to Ptahhotep, go ahead and instruct him in the Ancient Wisdom. May he become a model for the children of the great. May obedience enter into him, and may he be devoted to the one who speaks to him. No one is born wise.

And so begins the formulation of Mdw Nfr, *good speech,* to be spoken by the Prince, the Count, God's beloved, the eldest son of the Pharoah, the son of his body, Mayor of the City and Vizier, Ptahhotep, instructs the ignorant in the knowledge and in the standards of *good speech.* It will profit those who hear. It will be a loss to those who transgress. Ptahhotep began to speak to "Pharaoh's son" (to posterity).

1 Do not be proud and arrogant with your knowledge. Consult and converse with the ignorant and the wise, for the limits of artarenotreached. No artist ever possesses that perfection to which he should aspire. *Good speech* is more hidden than green• stone (emeralds), yet it may be found among maids at the grindstones.

2 If you meet a disputant in the heat of action, one who is more powerful than you, simply fold your arms and bend your back. To confront him will not make him agree with you. Pay no attention to his *evil*

speech. If you do not confront him while he is raging, people will call him an ignora• mus. Your self-control will be the match for his evil utterances.

3 If you meet a disputant in action, one who is your equal, one who is on your level, you will overcome him by being silent while he is speaking evilly. There will be much talk among those who hear and your name will be held in high regard among the great.

4 If you meet a disputant in action who is a poor man and who is not your equal do not attack him because he is weak. Leave him alone. He will confound himself. Do not answer him just so that you can relieve your own heart. Do not vent yourself against your opponent. Wretched is he who injures a poor man. If you ignore him listeners will wish to do what your want. You will beat him through their reproof.

5 If you are a man who leads, a man who controls the affairs of many, then seek the most perfect way of performing your re• sponsibility so that your conduct will be blameless. Great is Maat (truth, justice and righteousness). It is everlasting. Maat has been unchanged since the time of Asar. To create obstacles to the following of laws, is to open a way to a condition of violence. The transgressor of laws is pun• ished, although the greedy person over• looks this. Baseness may obtain riches, yet crime never lands its wares on the shore. In the end only Maat lasts. Man says, "Maat is my father's ground."¹¹

6 Do not scheme against people. God will punish accordingly; If a man says, "I shall live by scheming," he will lack bread for his mouth. If a man says, "I will be rich," he will have to say, "My cleverness has trapped me." If he says, "I will trap for myself" he will not be able to say, "I trapped for my profit." If a man says, "I will rob someone," he will end by being given to a stranger. People's schemes do not prevail. God's command is what prevails. There• fore, live in the midst of peace. What God £ives comes by itself.

7 If you are one among guests at the table of a person who is more powerful than you, take what that person gives just as it is set before you. Look at what is before you.

Don't stare at your host. Don't speak to him until he asks. One does not know what may displease him. Speak when he has spoken to you. Then your words will please the heart. The man who has plenty of the means of existence acts as his Ka commands. He will give food to those who he favors. It is the Ka that makes his hand stretch out. The great man gibes to the chosen man, thus eating is under the direction of God. It is a fool who complains about it.

8 If your are a person of trust sent by one great person to another great person, be careful to stick to the essence of the mes• sage that you were asked to transmit. Give the message exactly as he gave it to you. Guard against provocative speech which makes one great person angry with an• other. Just keep to the truth. Do not exceed it. However, even though there may have been an out-burst in the message you ^should not repeat it. Do not malign any• one, great or small, the Ka abhors it.

9 If you plow and if there is growth in your field and God lets it prosper in your hand, don't boast to your neighbor. One has

great respect for the silent person. A per•
son of character is a person of wealth. If that
person robs, he or she is like a crocodile in
the middle of the waters. If God gives you
children, don't impose on one who has no
children. Neither should you decry or brag
about having your own children, for there
is many a father who has grief and many a
mother with children who is less content
than another. It is the lonely whom God
nurtures while the family man prays for a
follower.

10 If you are poor, then serve a person of worth
so that your conduct may be well with God. Do
not bring up the fact that he was once poor. Do
not be arrogant towards him just because you
know about his former state. Respect him now
for his position of authority. As for fortune, it
obeys its own law and that is her will. It is God's
gift. It is God who makes him worthy and who
protects him while he sleeps, or who can turn
away from him.

11 Follow your heart as long as you live. Do no
more than is required. Do not shorten the time
of "follow the heart", since that offends the Ka.
Don't waste time on daily

cares over and beyond providing for your household. When wealth finally comes, then follow your heart. Wealth does no good if you are glum.

12 If you are a wise man, train up a son who will be pleasing to God. If he is straight and takes after you take good care of him. Do everything that is good for him. He is your son, your Ka begot him. Don't withdraw your heart from him. But an offspring can make trouble. If your son strays and neglects your council and dis• obeys all that is said, with his mouth spouting evil speech, then punish him for all his talk. God will hate him who crosses you. His guilt was determined in the womb. He who God makes boatless can• not cross the water,

13 If you are a guard in the storehouse, stand or sit rather than leave your post and trespass into someone else's place. Follow this rule from the first. Never leave your post, even when fatigued. Keen is the face to him who enters announced, and spa• cious is the seat of him who has been asked to come in. The storehouse has fixed rules. All behavior is strictly by the rule.

Only a God can penetrate the secure ware•
house where the rules are followed, even by
privileged persons.

14 If you are among the people then gain your
supporters by building trust. The trusted man is
one who does not speak the first thing that comes
to mind; and he will become a leader. A man of
means has a good name, and his face is benign.
People will praise him even without his knowl•
edge. On the other hand, he whose heart obeys
his belly asks for contempt of him• self in the
place of love. His heart is naked. His body is un-
anointed. The greathearted is a gift of God. He
who is ruled by his appetite belongs to the enemy.

15 Report the thing that you were commis•
sioned to report without error. Give your advice in the high council. If you are fluent in your
speech, it will not be hard for you to report. Nor
will anyone say of you, "who is he to know
this?" As to the au• thorities, their affairs will
fail if they punish you for speaking truth. They
should be silent upon hearing the report that
you have rendered as you have been told.

16 If you are a man who leads, a man whose authority reaches widely, then you should do perfect things, those which posterity will remember. Don't listen to the words of flatterers or to words that puff you up with pride and vanity.

17 If you are a person who judges, listen carefully to the speech of one who pleads. Don't stop the person from telling you everything that they had planned to tell you. A person in distress wants to pour out his or her heart, even more than they want their case to be won. If you are one who stops a person who is pleading, that person will say "why does he reject my plea?" Of course not all that one pleads for can be granted, but a good hearing soothes the heart. The means for getting a true and clear explanation is to listen with kindness.

18 If you want friendship to endure in the house that you enter, the house of a mas• ter, of a brother or of a friend, then in what ever place you enter beware of ap• proaching the women there. Unhappy is the place where this is done. Unwelcome is he who intrudes on them. A thousand men are turned away from their good because of a short moment that is like a dream, and then that moment is followed by death that comes from having known that dream. Anyone who encourages you to take advantage of the situation gives you poor advice. When you go to do it, your heart says no. If you are one who fails through the lust of women, then no affair of yours can prosper.

19 If you want to have perfect conduct, to be free from every evil, then above all guard against the vice of greed. Greed is a grievous sickness that has no cure. There is no treatment for it. It embroils fathers, mothers and the brothers of the mother. It parts the wife from the husband. Greed is a compound of all the evils. It is a bundle of all hateful things. That person endures whose rule is Tightness, who walks a straight line, for that person will leave a legacy by such behavior. On the other hand, the greedy has no tomb.

20 Do not be greedy in the division of things. Do not covet more than your share. Don't be greedy towards your relatives. A mild person has a greater claim than the harsh one. Poor is the person who forgets his relatives. He is deprived of their com• pany. Even a little bit of what is wanted will turn a quarreler into a friendly person.

21 When you prosper and establish your home, love your wife with ardor. Then fill her belly and clothe her back. Caress her. Give her ointments to soothe her body. Fulfill her wishes for as long as you live. She is a fertile field for her husband. Do not be brutal. Good manners will influence her better than force. Do not contend with her in the courts. Keep her from the need to resort to outside powers. Her eye is her storm when she gazes. It is by such treat• ment that she will be compelled to stay in your house.

22 Help your friends with things that you have, for you have these things by the grace of God. If you fail to help your friends, one will say you have a selfish Ka. One plans for tomorrow, but you do not know what tomorrow will bring. The right soul is the soul by which one is sustained. If you do praiseworthy deeds your friends will say, "welcome" in your time of need.

23 Don't repeat slander nor should you even listen to it. It is the spouting of the hot bellied. Just report a thing that has been observed, not something that has been heard secondhand. If it is something negligible, don't even say anything. He who is standing before you will recognize your worth. Slander is like a terrible dream against which one covers the face.

24 If you are a man of worth who sits at the council of a leader, concentrate on being excellent. Your silence is much better than boasting. Speak when you know that you have a solution. It is the skilled person who should speak when in council. Speaking is harder than all other work. The one who understands this makes speech a servant.

25 If you are mighty and powerful then gain respect through knowledge and through your gentleness of speech. Don't order things except as it is fitting. The one who provokes others gets into trouble. Don't be haughty lest you be humbled. But also don't be mute lest you be chided. When you answer one who is fuming, turn your face and control yourself. The flame of the hot hearted sweeps across every thing. But he who steps gently, his path is a paved road. He who is agitated all day has no happy moments but he who amuses himself all day can't keep his fortune.

26 Do not disturb a great man or distract his attention when he is occupied, trying to understand his task. When he is thus oc• cupied, he strips his body through the love of what he does. Love for the work which they do brings men closer to God. These are the people who succeed in what they do.

27 Teach the great what is useful to them. Be an aide to the great before the people. If you let your knowledge impress your leader, your substenance from him will then come from his soul. As his favorite's belly is filled, so will your back be clothed and his help will be there to sustain you. For your leader whom you love and who *lives* by useful knowledge, he in turn will give you good support. Thus will the love of you endure in his belly. He is a soul who loves to listen.

28 If you are an official of high standing, and you are commissioned to satisfy the many, then hold to a straight line. When you speak don't lean to one side or to the other. Beware lest someone complain, saying to the judges, "he has distorted things", and then your very deeds will turn into a judgment of you.

29 If you are angered by a misdeed, then lean toward a man on account of his Tightness. Pass over the misdeed and don't remem• ber it, since God was silent to you on the first day of your misdeed.

30 If you are great after having been humble, if you have gained your wealth after having been poor, and then go to a town that you know and that knows your former condition, don't put your trust in your newly acquired wealth which has come to you as a gift of God. If you do, one day someone there who is poor may very well overtake you.

31 Accept the authority of your leaders then your house will endure in its wealth. Your rewards will come from the right place. Wretched is he who opposes his   leader.

32 One lives as long as he is mild. Baring your arm does not hurt it. Do not plunder your neighbor's house or steal the goods of one that is near you, lest he denounce you before you are even heard. One who is argumentative is a mildless person. If he is also known as an aggressor, then that hostile man will have trouble in the neighborhood.

Be circumspect in matters of sexual rela• tions.

33 If you examine the character of a friend, don't ask other people, approach your friend. Deal with him alone, so as not to suffer from his anger. You may argue with him after a little while. You may test his heart in conversation. If what he has seen escapes him, if he does something that annoys you, stay friendly with him and do not attack. Be restrained and don't answer him with hostility. Do not leave him and do not attack him. His time will not fail to come. He cannot escape his fate.

34 Be generous as long as you live. What leaves the storehouse does not return. It is the food in the storehouse that one must share that is coveted. One whose belly is empty becomes an accuser. One who is deprived becomes an opponent. Therefore, do not have an accuser or an opponent as a neighbor. Your kindness to your neigh• bors will be a memorial to you for years, after you satisfy their needs.

35 Know your friends and then you prosper. Don't be mean towards your friends. They are like a watered field and greater than any material riches that you may have, for what belongs to one belongs to another. The character of one who is well born should be a profit to him. Good nature is a memorial.

36 Punish firmly and chastise soundly, then repression of crime becomes an example. But punishment except for crime will turn the complainer into an enemy.

37 If you take for a wife a good time woman who is joyful and who is well known in the town, if she is fickle and seems to live for the moment, do not reject her. Let her eat. The joyful person brings happiness.

38 If you listen to my saying all of your affairs will go forward. Their value resides in their truth. The memory of these sayings goes on in the speech of men and women because of the worth of their precepts. If every word is carried on, they will not perish in this land. If advice is given for the good, the great will speak accordingly. This is a matter of teaching a person to speak to posterity. He or she who hears it becomes a master hearer. It is good to speak to posterity. Posterity will listen.

If an example is set by him or her who leads, he or she will be beneficent forever, his wisdom lasting for all time. The wise person feeds the Ka with what endures, so that it is happy with that person on earth. The wise is known by his good actions. The heart of the wise matches his or her tongue and his or her lips are straight when he or she speaks. The wise have eyes that are made to see and ears that are made to hear what will profit the offspring. The wise person who acts with Maat is free of falsehood and disorder. Useful is hearing to a son who hears. If hearing enters the hearer, then the hearer be• comes a listener.

39 Hearing well is speaking well. Useful is hearing to one who hears. Hearing is better than every thing else. It creates good will. How good it is for a son to understand his father's

words. That son will reach old age through those words.

He who hears is beloved of God. He whom God hates does not hear. The heart makes of its owner a hearer or a non-hearer. Man's heart is his life, prosperity and health. The hearer is one who hears what is said. He who loves to hear is one who acts on what is said. How good it is for a son to listen to his father. How happy is he to whom it is said "Your son, is a master of hearing." The hearer of whom this is said is well endowed indeed and is honored by his father. That hearer's remembrance is in the mouth of the living, those that are on earth and those who will be.

40 If a man's son accepts his father's words then no plan of his will go wrong. So teach your son to be a hearer, one who will be valued by the officials, one who will guide his speech by what he has been told, one who is regarded as a hearer. This son will excel and his deeds will stand out while failure will follow those who do not hear. The wise wakes up early to his lasting gain while the fool is hard pressed.

41 The fool who does not hear, he can do nothing at all. He looks at ignorance and sees knowledge. He looks at harmfulness and sees usefulness. He does everything that one detests and is blamed for it every day. He lives on the things by which one dies. His food is evil speech.

His sort is known to the officials who say, "There goes a living death every day." One ignores the things that he does because of his many daily troubles.

45 A son who hears is a follower of Heru. When he is old and has reached the period where he is venerated, then he will speak likewise to his own children, renewing then the teachings of his father.

Every man teaches as he acts. He will speak to the children so that they will speak to their children. He will set an example and not give offense. So if justice stands firm, your chil• dren will live. As to the first child who gets into trouble, when people see it, they will say about the child "that is just like him", and they will also say when they even hear a rumor about the child, "that is just like him too."

To see everyone is to satisfy the many. Any riches that you have are useless without the many. Don't say something and then take it back. Don't put one thing in place of another. Beware of releasing the restraints in you, least the wise man say, "listen, if you want to endure in the mouth of the hearers, speak after you have mastered the craft." If you speak to good purpose all your affairs will be in place.

46 Conceal your heart. Control your mouth. Then you will be known among the officials. Be quite exact before your leader. Act so that no one will say to him "he is the son of that one."

Be deliberate when you speak so as to say things that count. Then the officials who listen will say, "how good is the thing that comes from his mouth."

47 Act so that your leader will say of you, "how good is he whom his father has taught. When he came forth from his body, he told him all that was in his mind, and he does even more than he was told."

The good son is the gift of God and exceeds what is told him by his leader. He will do right when his heart is straight. As you succeed me sound in body, a Pharaoh, content with all that was done, may you obtain many years of life.

The things that I did on earth were not small. I have had 110 years of life. As a gift of the Pharaoh, I have had honors exceeding those of the ancestors, by doing Maat until the state of veneration.

It is done, from its beginning to its end, as it was found in the writings of the ancestors and Deity.

CPSIA information can be obtained
at www.ICGtesting.com
Printed in the USA
LVHW082110030123
736373LV00004B/905

9 781532 939990